THE HIP-HOP REVOLUTION

CHANCE THE RAPPER
MAKING MUSIC AND GIVING BACK

TOM HEAD AND
DEIRDRE HEAD

Enslow Publishing
101 W. 23rd Street
Suite 240
New York, NY 10011
USA

enslow.com

Published in 2020 by Enslow Publishing, LLC.

101 W. 23rd Street, Suite 240, New York, NY 10011

Library of Congress Cataloging-in-Publication Data

Names: Head, Tom, author. | Head, Deirdre, author.
Title: Chance the Rapper : making music and giving back / Tom Head and Deirdre Head.
Description: New York : Enslow Publishing, 2020. | Series: The hip-hop revolution | Audience: 5 | Includes bibliographical references and index.
Identifiers: LCCN 2018046992| ISBN 9781978509641 (library bound) | ISBN 9781978510067 (pbk.) | ISBN 9781978510074 (6 pack)
Subjects: LCSH: Chance the Rapper—Juvenile literature. | Rap musicians—United States—Biography—Juvenile literature.
Classification: LCC ML3930.C442 H42 2020 | DDC 782.421649092 [B] —dc23
LC record available at https://lccn.loc.gov/2018046992

Printed in the United States of America

To Our Readers: We have done our best to make sure all websites in this book were active and appropriate when we went to press. However, the author and the publisher have no control over and assume no liability for the material available on those websites or on any websites they may link to. Any comments or suggestions can be sent by email to customerservice@enslow.com.

CONTENTS

BECOMING
THE RAPPER

C hance the Rapper was born Chancelor Bennett on April 16, 1993. He was born and raised in Chicago. His father, Ken, worked for Chicago mayor Harold Washington. Later, Ken worked for Senator Barack Obama in Illinois. After Senator Obama became president, Ken worked in the Department of Labor. Chance's mother, Lisa, worked for the Illinois attorney general's office. She also owned a tobacco farm in North Carolina. Chance has a younger brother, Taylor. Chance's parents achieved much in their lives. They had high hopes for their sons.

Chance and Taylor grew up in West Chatham. West Chatham is a middle-class neighborhood in Chicago's mostly black South Side. Chance loved music, but he didn't grow up with rap. This changed when Chance was eleven years old. Kanye West's debut album, *The College Dropout,* came out, and Chance loved it. Chance especially loved "Through the Wire." Kanye recorded "Through the Wire" while his jaw was wired shut after a car accident. After that, Chance didn't just listen to rap. He rapped himself. He also shared mixtapes of other local teenage rappers. He learned from them and won them new fans.

Chance the Rapper attends the 2017 BET Awards, where he won for New Artist, Collaboration, Album of the Year, and the Humanitarian Award.

In his mid-teens, Chance performed often as a rapper. He drew crowds all over the South Side. He was known for his unusual sense of humor.

RAPPER OR LAWYER?

Ken introduced his sons to President Obama. At the time, Chance and his father had been arguing about

Chance's future career. Ken asked his son not to tell the president he wanted to be a rapper. Instead, he had him say he wanted to be a lawyer. This led to a period of time when Ken and his son rarely spoke to each other. They could not agree about Chance's future.

By 2011, the people around Chance knew he wanted to build a career as a rapper. Whether he would succeed was another matter. After Chance was suspended from high school for marijuana possession, his future didn't look so bright. But like so many artists before him, he took a bad experience and made art out of it. He used the time off from school to begin work on his first mixtape. He called it *10 Day*, named after the ten-day

Instrumentality

As a teenager, Chance (who went by Chano) rapped with his friend Justin (who went by J-Emcee). They called their group Instrumentality. They released more than fifty songs. One single, "Good Enough," talked about how they were rejected by a record company. "Good Enough" was very popular in Chicago.

Clive Davis

Chance the Rapper is photographed with his parents, Lisa and Ken Bennett, at the pre-Grammy gala in Beverly Hills, California, on February 11, 2017.

suspension. After he returned to school, he kept working on his songwriting. He also performed when he could.

TALENT AND TRAGEDY

Chance's life changed on the night of September 3, 2011. He and a close friend, a fellow rapper named Rodney

Chance the Rapper performs at the Meadows Music and Arts Festival in Queens, New York, on October 2, 2016. His dreams of becoming a successful rapper were realized.

Kyles Jr., were walking home from a house party. They accidentally bumped into a tall, stocky white stranger. The stranger stabbed Kyles to death, then fled.

Later that night, Chance and his father had a long talk. They agreed that Chance would have a year to become a successful rapper. If he couldn't, he would go to college.

Kyles was one of three friends Chance lost that year. It affected his outlook. His concerts became sharper, more energetic, and more vulnerable. By the time he released *10 Day* online that next April, Chance had grown up. He was a young artist wrestling in public with his fear, his grief, and his anger. He had a lot to say. Millions of people were about to listen.

Six months later, a *Forbes* magazine article caught Ken's eye. It said Chance had become one of the top ten independent artists. Ken had to admit that his son had met his end of the bargain. Ken also knew that, as his father, he had to support his son's career.

"I'm a rapper! You should be able to say that . . . and, like, make someone scared in a good way."[1]

MAKING HISTORY

2

C hance began 2012 as a young man with big dreams. He was already well-known in Chicago for his rap performances. He would soon release his first full-length mixtape, *10 Day*.

Most artists secure a recording contract and release a debut album. Chance did things differently. He releases mixtapes, not albums. As he and J-Emcee had rapped on their local Chicago single "Good Enough," major record labels make new artists think they're not talented enough to sign up. Chance wanted to release music in a way that was more accessible to everybody. He released *10 Day* for free over the internet.

Chance calls *10 Day* a mixtape rather than an album because mixtapes have always been free or cheap. Mixtapes are collections of songs given out by rappers

Acid Rap

Chance had become a major artist. But he still released his second mixtape, *Acid Rap*, for free online in April 2013. It received more than a million downloads on the mixtape-sharing site Datpiff alone.[1]

or DJs to promote their work. People are usually grateful to their friends for listening to their mixtapes. Chance was truly grateful that people were interested in his music. He didn't want them to have to pay for it.

Chance visits the *Sway in the Morning* SiriusXM radio show on June 19, 2013, to discuss his *Acid Rap* mixtape.

BECOMING A SUPERSTAR

Chance's Chicago fans already knew he was talented. *10 Day* showed the rest of the world. He released his third free mixtape, *Coloring Book*, in 2016. Chance showed that his talent could mix well with the rest of the hip-hop community. Most of the tracks were

Chance performed with his idol, Kanye West, at the Magnificent Coloring Day Festival in Chicago on September 24, 2016. Chance organized the festival, which featured such artists as John Legend, Alicia Keys, and Skrillex.

collaborations with older, more established artists, such as 2 Chainz, Lil Wayne, Young Thug, and Future. He recorded a song with Christian gospel performer Kirk Franklin. He was even able to work with his long-time role model Kanye West on "All We Got." They rapped over vocals from their hometown Chicago Children's Choir.

Chance was only twenty-three years old when *Coloring Book* came out. But he had grown emotionally during his four years as a superstar. The anger and self-doubt fans heard on *10 Day* were still there in places.

> "I don't have to carry myself as anybody that I'm not, and people picked up on it."[2]

Yet so was a new confidence. His sometimes dark sense of humor was still present on *Coloring Book*. However, here it was tempered by a gentle message of faith and hope. The mixtape is the most popular of Chance's projects so far, and it exposed him to a new audience.

A NEW KIND OF SUCCESS

Chance's fame also showed new artists that they didn't have to get a recording contract to achieve success. His

Chance makes his acceptance speech at the 59th Grammy Awards on February 12, 2017, after winning for Best Rap Album. He won three Grammys that year.

free online music showed a new generation of rappers that they could go directly to their fans to build an audience. He even won a Grammy Award for the mixtape. This made him the first internet-based artist to do so. By the end of 2016, Chance the Rapper wasn't just a successful rapper. He had redefined what success as a rapper meant.

Chance also kept himself busy by working with other rap artists and groups on their projects. His group, the Social Experiment, released the mixtape *Surf* on iTunes as an exclusive, free release. The album was downloaded more than 600,000 times.[3] The online magazine *Pitchfork* listed the work as one of the fifty best albums of the year. Some of the musical artists featured on the album with Chance were Janelle Monáe, Erykah Badu, and Busta Rhymes. Chance also appeared on singles by Justin Bieber, Big Sean, and John Legend.

CHICAGO'S CHAMPION

C hance donated one million dollars to Chicago's public schools in March 2017. He did this after the governor had vetoed $215 million in school funding.[1] Chance discussed the topic during a 2018 podcast at the Museum of Contemporary Art in Chicago. "I got to learn so much stuff: how we are the only [school] district in the state that doesn't have an elected school board," he said. "I got to see how different the facilities are on the South and West sides of the city from the ones on the North Side."[2]

Chance recognized that individual donations like his would not be enough. He called on Chicago's business community to take a more active role in funding the public school system. He also asked the governor to work with other political leaders to come up with long-term

Chance presents a check for one million dollars to Chicago's public schools on March 6, 2017. This marks the beginning of his charitable work.

school funding plans. Chance cofounded the organization SocialWorks. SocialWorks went on to raise another $2.2 million for the city's public schools later that year.[3] It has continued to raise money for the district ever since.

Chance got his start as a rapper during his own suspension from school. Now he had become a national advocate for the public school system.

"I'm not going anywhere. I'm gonna live in Chicago till the day I die."[4]

BUSINESS IS GOOD

Chance releases his music online for free, but he still earns a lot of money. His free mixtapes advertise his other projects. Several years ago, Chance began wearing a cap with the number 3 on it. This was to celebrate the release of his third mixtape, *Coloring Book*. The number

Chance wears his famous number 3 logo at the grand opening of the Great Wolf Lodge water park on June 21, 2018, in Gurnee, Illinois.

Chance's Trademark

Chance applied for a trademark in 2014. It was for the number 3 logo that's on his caps and other merchandise. To use his number 3 logo, companies must get his permission. This usually means giving him some of the profits.

3 holds other meanings for him as well. It's relevant to his faith as a reference to the Father, Son (Jesus Christ), and Holy Spirit in Christianity. It also refers to his new family: himself, his fiancée Kirsten Corley, and their daughter, Kensli. Kensli was born in September 2015.

Soon his fans began wearing caps with the number 3 on them, too. Chance allowed companies to sell official caps with the number 3 logo. Now he gets paid every time something with his number 3 design is sold. He makes millions of dollars off of concerts and merchandise. He has also begun an acting career.

CHANCE THE ACTOR

Even when he was a teenage rapper in Chicago, Chance's sense of humor was obvious. He's also very good at managing an audience. When he wants his fans to

Chance attends the *Slice* premiere with director Austin Vesely in Chicago on September 10, 2018. This is Chance's first major film.

be happy, they're happy. When he wants them to get serious, they get serious. These skills have made him a natural actor.

Chance won fans all over the world with his holiday guest spots on *Saturday Night Live*. His musical performance in 2016's "Jingle Barack (Last Christmas)," a funny skit, won him an Emmy Award. He hosted the show a year later for the 2017 Thanksgiving episode. Chance also went on MTV's live rap comedy series *Wild 'n Out*.

Chance starred in 2018's *Slice*. It is a comedy horror film set in a small town where pizza delivery people are being murdered. Chance plays a pizza delivery driver, a werewolf who is attempting to solve the crimes. The movie was directed by Austin Vesely. He had also directed two of Chance's music videos. Much like Chance's music, *Slice* was released online.

THE FUTURE OF CHANCE

For years, Chance has described his daughter's mother, Kirsten Corley, as his best friend and has credited her for much of his success. He proposed to her at a Fourth of July party in 2018.

Chance is determined to be a good father. He does not want his career to take away from his family life. But becoming a parent has had an effect on his music. "The content itself has changed," he told NPR in 2017. "[I'm] rapping as if I know she's going to listen. But also, I just can't be at the studio all night because I have a daughter. I'm more conscious of my time and I've come to understand that . . . art is awesome,

> "[Art is] just a reflection. The real thing is my daughter."

Chance and Kirsten Corley attend the Chicago Bulls vs. New Orleans Pelicans pre-season NBA game on October 8, 2017.

art is beautiful because it's a reflection of life and it describes life and shows life in its beauty. But it's just a reflection. The real thing is my daughter. I understand what is most important now."[1]

His faith has also played a more central role in his recent work. "I don't make Christian rap," he told *Teen Vogue*, "but I am a Christian rapper."[2]

TOURING THE WORLD

Chance balances his family life, songwriting, and fund-raising work with a busy tour schedule. Like his role model Kanye West, he enjoys working on many projects at the same time. In late 2018, Chance also pledged $1 million toward mental health services in Chicago.

Chance toured the United States shortly after winning his 2017 Grammy Awards. He did this to support *Coloring Book*. He called it the Be Encouraged Tour in keeping with the mixtape's Christian gospel roots. The tour was extremely successful. Venues often sold out. Still, Chance kept his family in Chicago a priority and visited them between concerts.

Chance began touring Asia in mid-2018. He continues to expand his audience all over the world.

A Special Concert

In July 2018, Chance organized and performed at a concert to celebrate the fiftieth anniversary of the Special Olympics in Chicago. The concert raised funds for future Special Olympics projects. In addition to Chance, it featured performances by R&B artists Usher and Smokey Robinson and pop-rock singer Jason Mraz.

Chance enjoyed performing in Chicago during his early years. He still does despite having millions of fans all over the world. He often comes back home to Chicago to rap.

On July 21, 2018, Chance the Rapper and several other artists celebrated the fiftieth anniversary of the Special Olympics.

Chance (*center*) and his younger brother, Taylor Bennett (*left*), laugh and have a good time at the 2017 Grammy Awards. Taylor is also a rapper.

THE NEXT IDEA

Even by his normal standards, 2018 was a busy year for Chance the Rapper. He released four rap tracks on their own, without a mixtape. These tracks were very popular. He also told fans that a fourth mixtape would be released soon.

On the fifth anniversary of *10 Day*'s release, *Okayplayer* magazine interviewed Dr. P. Joseph Powers. Dr. Powers was Chance's principal at Jones Prep High School. It was Dr. Powers who had suspended Chance for ten days for marijuana possession, inspiring the mixtape title. After thanking Chance for the work he'd done raising money for Chicago schools, Dr. Powers was asked if he had anything he'd like to pass on to his most famous student. "I would just tell him congratulations on the successes he has had," Dr. Powers answered, "and I wish him many more years of success."[3]

Chance still loves his home city of Chicago. He's still close to his parents. He's helping his younger brother start his own rap career. Despite this success, Chance has not lost touch with his roots.

TIMELINE

1993 Chance Bennett is born in Chicago on April 16.

2004 Kanye West's debut album, *College Dropout*, is released, igniting young Chance's interest in rap.

2008 Chance begins recording mixtapes with his high school friend Justin (J-Emcee). They perform under the name Instrumentality.

2011 Chance begins writing and recording *10 Day*, his first solo mixtape, during a ten-day suspension from high school.

2012 Chance releases *10 Day* online. This launches his national career.

2013 Chance releases *Acid Rap*.

2014 Chance receives the city of Chicago's annual Outstanding Youth Award.

2015 Along with four other musicians (who collectively call themselves the Social Experiment), Chance the Rapper releases *Surf*.

2015 Chance's daughter, Kensli, is born in September.

2016 Chance releases *Coloring Book*.

2016 Chance wins a BET Image Award for Best New Hip-Hop Artist.

2017 Chance wins Grammy Awards for Best New Artist and Best Rap Performance, as well as an NAACP Image Award for Outstanding New Artist.

2018 Chance becomes engaged to Kirsten Corley.

2018 Chance makes his film debut in the horror comedy *Slice*.

CHAPTER NOTES

CHAPTER 1. BECOMING THE RAPPER

1. Mark Anthony Green, "The Gospel According to Chance the Rapper," *GQ*, February 14, 2017, https://www.gq.com/story/chance-the-rapper-profile-2017.

CHAPTER 2. MAKING HISTORY

1. Billboard Staff, "The Evolution of Chance the Rapper," *Billboard*, October 6, 2016, https://www.billboard.com/articles/columns/hip-hop/7525638/the-evolution-of-chance-the-rapper.

2. Sami Yenigun, "Chance the Rapper on Mixtapes, Politics and Priorities," *The Record*, NPR, August 9, 2017, https://www.npr.org/sections/therecord/2017/08/09/542077601/chance-the-rapper-on-mixtapes-politics-and-priorities.

3. David Renshaw, "Chance the Rapper Reveals Over 600,000 People Have Already Downloaded His Free 'Surf' Album," *NME*, June 6, 2015, https://www.nme.com/news/music/chance-the-rapper-37-1210472.

CHAPTER 3. CHICAGO'S CHAMPION

1. Dakin Andone, "Chance the Rapper Donates $1 Million to Chicago Public Schools," CNN, August 16, 2017, https://www.cnn.com/2017/03/06/us/chance-the-rapper-donates-1-million-chicago-public-schools/index.html.

2. Resita Cox, "Chance the Rapper on Music, Black Women and His Love for Home: 'I'm Gonna Live in Chicago Till the Day I Die,'" The TRiiBE, March 6, 2018, https://thetriibe.com/2018/03/chance-the-rapper-in-sight-out-pitchfork-mca-chicago/.

3. Daniel Kreps, "Watch Chance the Rapper Announce $2.2 Million Fund for Chicago Schools," *Rolling Stone,* September 2, 2017, https://www.rollingstone.com/music/music-news/watch-chance-the-rapper-announce-2-2-million-fund-for-chicago-schools-126511/.

4. Cox.

CHAPTER 4. THE FUTURE OF CHANCE

1. Brian "Z" Zisook, "How Becoming a Parent Changed Chance's Approach to Making Music," DJBooth, August 9, 2017, https://djbooth.net/features/2017-08-09-chance-the-rapper-parenting.

2. Elaine Welteroth, ed., "Chance the Rapper Opens Up About What It's Like to Challenge Kanye West," *Teen Vogue,* May 16, 2017, https://www.teenvogue.com/story/chance-the-rapper-jordan-peele-cover-interview-music-issue-creativity.

3. Kevito, "As '10 Day' Celebrates Its 5th Anniversary, Chance's Principal Speaks Out [Interview]," *Okayplayer*, 2017, http://www.okayplayer.com/news/chance-rappers-former-principal-shares-thoughts-10-day-mixtape-anniversary.html.

GLOSSARY

accessible Easy to use, reach, or understand.

advocate A person who supports a cause.

attorney general A lawyer who works for the US government or a state government.

collaboration A project worked on by two or more people.

independent Without the help of a major record company.

merchandise Products associated with a celebrity.

mixtape A collection of songs recorded by a rapper or DJ, usually either given away for free or sold at a low cost.

profits Money made from a sale.

skit A short, funny performance piece.

tempered Made less severe.

track An individual piece of music recorded on an album or mixtape.

trademark A unique symbol or term that a person or company uses.

venue A place where events take place.

veto To reject.

vulnerable Easily hurt emotionally or physically.

FURTHER READING

BOOKS

Bailey, Diane. *Chance the Rapper: Independent Innovator*. Edina, MN: Essential Library, 2018.

Morgan, Joe L. *Hip Hop and R&B: Chance the Rapper*. Broomall, PA: Mason Crest, 2018.

Niver, Heather Moore. *Chance the Rapper: Hip-Hop Artist*. New York, NY: Enslow Publishing, 2018.

WEBSITES

Chance Raps
chanceraps.com
Visit Chance's official website, featuring his latest music releases and free archived mixtapes.

SocialWorks
socialworkschi.org
Learn more about Chance's nonprofit organization.

INDEX